How to Find and Get Permission to Hunt
GHOST TOWNS!

By

Frank Hayslip

Printed in the United States of America

Cover Design & Photos: Frank Hayslip

fhayslip@cox.net
www.fhayslip.com

TWIN TERRITORY BOOK PRODUCTIONS
6036 NW 47TH
WARR ACRES, OKLAHOMA 73122

CONTENTS

What Is A Ghost Town?

Here in Oklahoma there are over 5000 ghost town sites. Most were created during the land run of 1889 when thousands of people gathered to run for the rich fertile soil of the plains. People would soon gather in a small community, someone would build a store, a livery, and before long they had the beginning of a town. They would try to lure the railroad near their town for without it the farmers would have a hard time delivering their crops to market. Without the railroads, the town would slowly die and many did.

Ghost towns in Oklahoma and many other states are not like what you see in the movies. You probably won't see many weather-beaten buildings about to fall down, tumbleweeds rolling down the street, or a saloon with tables and bottles setting on top of them. Maybe in the high western mountains you might run across one of them, but don't expect this type of place. In Oklahoma you'll usually find one of three things:

The First Thing you may find is someone has built a building or house on the town site. Most folks in the country don't want anyone to dig in their front yard, but sometimes you can get permission but don't ask with the shovel in your hand. Ask if they know where the town once stood, and if they do it may save a lot of unnecessary digging.

If it had been a large town the area around the farm house would be a good place to hunt, and the nearby fields. Houses would be spread out and as you know where people congregate things have a tendency to be lost. Ask the farmer if he has noticed broken glass or brick in his field and that's the first place I'd search.

You'll be surprised how many people never realized there was ever a town located on their property. It may get them thinking about those bricks in the field, or that strange well in the south forty. Ask and you may receive a welcome answer. Remember roads back then may not be the same roads they have today, but somewhere in that section you'll find the town.

The Second Thing you may find is a plowed field. This will be a good and bad place to hunt. The good thing is it will be easy to dig and you should be able to see broken pieces of glass, brick and other debris on top of the ground, and maybe a few coins. And every time they plow it will be like a new place. Things will be brought to the surface while other things will be buried deeper. It's almost impossible to hunt out a place like this.

One ghost town that I hunted, the land owner told me an employee who used to plow the site would always bring his wife with him. She would walk behind the plow and pick up the coins he dug up. This was the first time I'd ever heard anything like this because you usually you don't find that many coins in a ghost town. Later in my research, I found out this town would have a street dance every Saturday night and hundreds of people would attend. They laid straw in the muddy streets and if someone dropped anything in the straw and mud it quickly disappeared. With all the dancing and joy juice consumed many things were lost under the mud.

On one trip to this ghost town I found four barber quarters, twelve barber dimes, sixteen v nickels, ten Indian head pennies and eight tokens. I was having a field day until the descending sun forced me to leave. Whenever I thought I had found it all, they would plow it again and it became a new site. If you find a good site like this, search it again and again until you come up empty. Why go somewhere else when you're finding goodies? The bad thing about these sites is things will be scattered everywhere and some of the things will be damaged by the plow, but it's still a great place to hunt.

The Third Thing you may find and what I think is the idea site is a large pasture that has never seen the plow. When you find the town site things will be in a confined area. A site like this will be very productive and most things will not be damaged. Those beautiful coins will be only a few inches deep.

At the base of this mountain is the ghost town of Coon Hollow.

How to Find a Ghost Town Site

For many years people have asked me how I find ghost town sites and get permission to hunt. So I've decided to put together a simply guide for you to follow that will put you on a ghost town site.

People who have just started to metal detect usually hunt parks, school yards, fair grounds, and this is fine because it gives you experience on how to use your metal detector and that wonderful acceleration of digging up that first coin.

But to find the really old stuff, you need to be where people lived a long time ago. Research is very imitating to people and most don't know where to begin. There are a lot of books on this subject but it consumes a lot of time. This is not to say you shouldn't do research for eventually you will, but there is a much easier way to find ghost towns that I think will be more beneficial to you as a beginner.

With this guide, two books and a county map, you can be on a ghost town site today. If barber quarters, dimes, Indian head pennies, V and buffalo nickels is your ideal of metal detecting, then ghost town hunting should be right up your alley. This book was written primarily for Oklahoma hunters but it can be used for other states as well.

Warning! Once you hunt a ghost town, you'll be a ghost town hunter forever.

I use two books and a county map to locate any ghost town in that county. The first book is titled: "OKLAHOMA PLACE NAMES" by George H. Shirk. $9.95 (Many other states have place name books so you can apply this to them also) this book lists over 5000 ghost towns along with a brief history. It may also tell you how it got its name, the years it had a post office which will tell you approximately how long the town existed.

I usually don't hunt a ghost town unless it's been in existent for at least ten years. I seem to be able to find more things in them rather than one who's only existed for a few years.

After reading a brief history of the town and if I decide to try to search it, I use a book titled: "TOWN AND PLACE LOCATIONS" The key word on this book is LOCATIONS. It doesn't give you any information about the towns, but it will give you the exact location within a square mile, the name of the town, county, range, township, and section number. You can purchase this book at the Oklahoma Department of Highways and you can also purchase the county maps. A single county map cost around $1.00 and you can buy a complete set of all the counties for around $60.00. If you're going to hunt a lot of ghost towns, I suggest you buy the complete set.

There's nothing like wanting to search a ghost town but you don't have a map for that county and the Oklahoma Department of Highways is closed. Buy the maps!

So with these two books and a county map you can locate any town that existed in that county. Be sure to mark more than one town site on your map for there may be a reason you can't get on some of them. Like if the farmer has crops in the field, or you can't find the land owner. Please do not enter without permission. Many places are now off limits because someone has trespassed, and didn't fill their holes.

On the map I'll look for water, a creek or river. Most of the towns are located near water and most are built on a four way corner. In the mountains this is not the case, but there should be a road, trail, or path that will lead you to the site.

I'll begin my search on the four way corner and look for broken glass, brick, iron, tin and other debris that will help me determine the site. If you can't find the site, don't panic, the search is not over. The next step is to get permission to enter the property.

(This is the site of "Keokuk Falls" (1892-1918)

Keokuk Falls was one of the toughest frontier towns. It had three hotels, two distilleries, ten doctors, seven saloons and one coffin factory. There never was a marshal or lawman. It was know as the home of the "Seven deadly saloons" it was reported that one stagecoach driver told his passengers "Stop twenty minutes and see a man die."

This is all that's left of the old ghost town of Howdy, Okla.

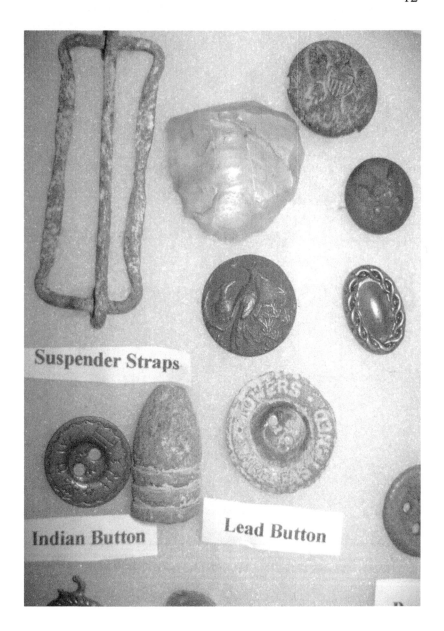

Suspender Straps

Indian Button

Lead Button

How to Get Permission

At this point some people go to the court house, look up the property owner, his address and get permission, but this takes a lot of time and there's a much better way.

Look For The Nearest House If they are not the land owner, you can bet your bottom dollar they know who is for farm folks know who owns what and whether they'll shoot you or invite you to dinner.

If a woman answers the door, never ask permission because she will always tell you to talk to her husband. The only exception is if she's a widow.

I'll start out the conversation by introducing myself and then I'll say,

"I've been doing some research on an old ghost town (name the town) and I understand it was located on this property. Can you tell me anything about it?"

By doing this, you've told him who you are, why you're there, and all you're asking for is a little information. Farm folks like to talk about the past and this puts them at ease and if they know anything about the town they'll tell you. How many stores were there, how many people, saloons, and who got drunk on Saturday night.

Sometimes they'll tell you about another place you may want to search later. I found an unknown army camp this way and it was very productive.

I always ask if they know where the town stood. If they do, it will save a lot of searching. After I get all the information I can I'll then ask who the land owner is, where he lives, and if possible his phone number. I have a cell phone I carry with me and sometimes I'll call the owner if I'm short on time, but it's better to talk to him in person if you can.

After I find the land owner I'll say, "I like to hunt ghost towns with a metal detector to see if I can find something with the name of the town on it."

At this point I'll ask if he knows what a metal detector is and if he doesn't I'll explain it to him. I never say, "Can I have permission?" this leaves it too easy for him to say no, so I'll say,

"Would you mind if I go on your property with a metal detector and see what I can find?"

By asking him, "Would you mind? You've put the impression in his mind that you think it's alright but you just wanted to be sure. It makes it awful hard for him to say no by asking this way. I have asked many different ways, but this seems to work better than anything else.

I'll explain what I'm going to do, fill up all my holes, carry out all the trash I dig up and leave the area exactly like I found it. After receiving permission, I'll say,

"If I find anything interesting, I'll come back and show you."

Most folks are interested in what you find but not because they want anything, but they always seem to be interested in seeing it. In all the places I've hunted, I've only had one man who wanted something that I found. It was a 1905 Indian head penny and the reason he wanted it was because that was the year he was born. But remember, if you happen to find an 1888 gold coin, you'll be surprised how many people were born in that year.

There are two reasons I always show the things I find to the land owner.

The First Reason is to get them interested in what I'm doing which makes them part of the hunt. When you do this, you're no longer a stranger and if you're not a stranger things get a whole lot better. Like how about a piece of pie or get invited for dinner. Both of these things have happen to me.

The Second Reason is if I want to come back. Believe me, if you find some neat things you will want to come back. Sometimes on my second or third trip is when I find the best things because I've carried off the trash on the first trip that masked my target. After showing the land owner what I've found and offering him anything I've found I'll say,
"I really appreciate you allowing me to go on your property and I had a great time. Would you mind if I come back some other time?"
After I receive permission I'll say,
"I have a friend who sometimes goes hunting with me, would you mind if I bring him with me?"
If he says yes the next thing I'll ask for is his gold watch. (Just kidding)
So now you're set, you've got permission to come back and you can bring your hunting buddy with you. Sometimes I'll make up a display of some of the things I found and give it to the land owner. Each time they seem to be shocked that I found these things in his field and a few of them have told me to come back anytime. Don't you just love to hear that?
Because of vandalism, someone leaving a gate open and property being stolen, you'll probably see a lot of no trespassing signs.

Don't let No Trespassing Signs Intimidate You.

These signs are not put up to keep you out, but to keep people out who hasn't received permission.
In 1982 I went to an old ghost town in the country called, "Keokuk Falls." When I arrived at the site there were signs all over his fence. "No Trespassing! Keep Out! Trespassers Will Be Shot! Guarded By Smith & Wesson!" It looked like a billboard. To make matters worse the

fellow who lived across the road said the owner had ran two men off his property who were metal detecting without permission two weeks ago. I really hated to hear this.

I almost left but it was such a long drive I decided to ask anyway. He may shoot me, but he can't eat me that's against the law... ain't it?

After knocking on the door and expecting to see a giant of a man I was surprised when an elderly lady answered the door. I asked to speak to her husband and she said he was plowing the field behind the house. I walked up to the fence and the farmer was at the end of the field and just turned around and started plowing toward me.

A million thoughts ran though my mind as I waited for him. What am I going to say to him to convince him to let me on his property? My mind said, "Stay! Stay!" but my feet said, "Run! Run!" Fortunately my mind won the battle which is strange because my mind usually don't win any battles.

He pulled up and turned off his tractor. I took a deep breath and quickly said,

"I don't know my name, but I'd like to talk to you."
Realizing what I said, I quickly corrected myself.

"No! I know my name!" He began to smile as I spoke at a rapid pace.

"I understand the old ghost town of Keokuk Falls is on your property and I wonder if you would mind if I went on there with a metal detector and see what I could find. I promise I'll fill all my holes, carry off all the trash and I'll even plant some seeds if you want me to."

I must have turned green or something because he was almost laughing.

"I see you've seen my signs."

"Yes sir I did!" I rattled out.

"I put up those signs to keep people off my property who don't have permission to be there. I don't mind folks on my property as long as I know what they're doing. Just like you wouldn't want folks in your back yard without permission I don't either. I have no problem with you going out there with a metal detector and I appreciate you coming and asking. You go right ahead and I hope you find something. Just let me know when you leave."

He was a very nice man nothing like what I expected. I've told you that to tell you this;

Don't Let No Trespassing Signs Intimidate You!

If you have permission, the signs don't mean anything. Follow this simple guide and you can be on a ghost town site today and the hunt will be one you'll never forget.

If you happen to be out hunting a ghost town and see an old gray-haired fellow carrying a metal detector, a shovel, looking like he's lost, say hello, it may be me.

Remember, don't damage anything, close gates, be sure to fill your holes, carry out all the trash you dig and treat the property like it was your own, and you'll have no problem. Good luck and I hope all your beepers be keepers.

What Do You Expect To Find In Ghost Towns?

The next few pages will show you what I've found in ghost towns.

Suspender Straps

utton Cir: 1855-1902

Enlisted Man's Button Cir: 1854 – 1902

Brass Tent Peg

Carved Lead Heart

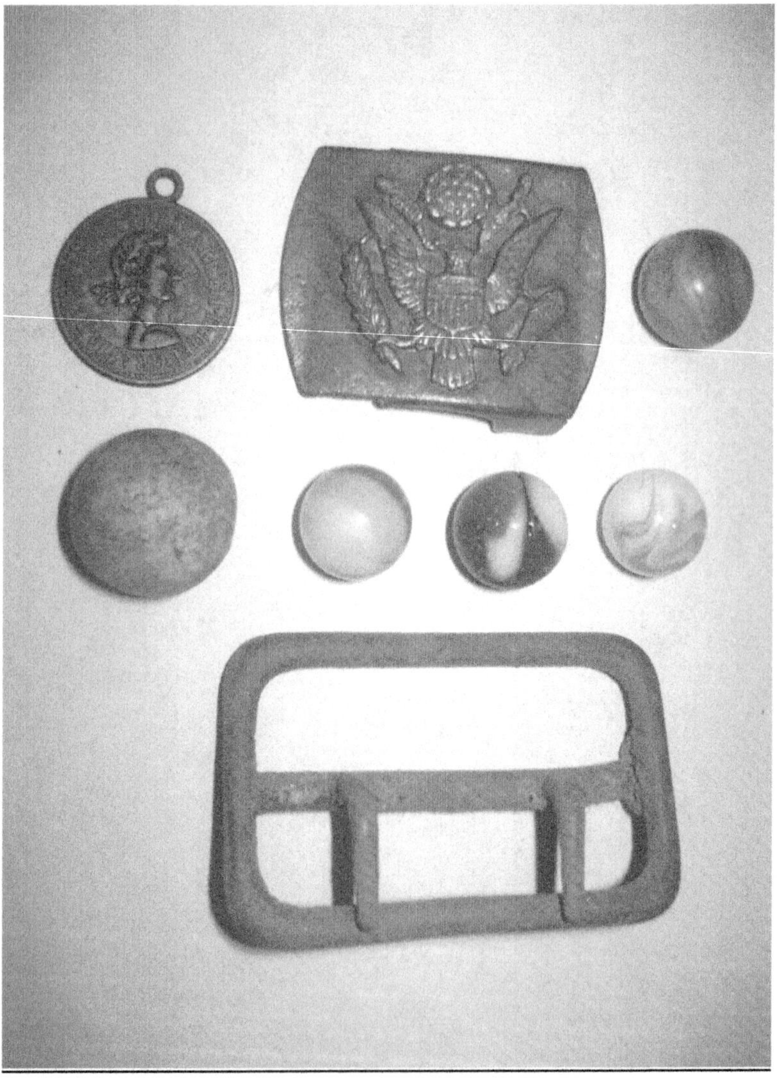

9,1873

Lady's Suspender Strap Pat. 12-13, 1892

This old hand pump survived the years but the town of Mill Creek vanished. Post office established June 11, 1879
(That's me with the landowners hound dog, he helped me hunt)

This beautiful lady sometimes goes with me, my wife Elsie

This display give me permission to come back anytime

How to Read a County Map

Some of you may not know how to read a county map, but it's really not that hard. I'll try to explain it to you.

There are <u>36 square mile sections</u> in a township. The first one is numbered #1 on the map. The other numbers will be #6 #31 and #36. The other sections are not numbered. (Refer to the map on page 27)
Notice on the top of the map the letters: (R 13 E) this is the <u>Range.</u> On the left and right side are the letters: (T 2 N) this is the <u>Township.</u>

Suppose you're trying to find the town of Pine, and the directions are: (Section 22 - R 13 E - T 2 N) simply place your finger on <u>R 13 W</u> and place your other finger on <u>T 2 N</u>. Where your two fingers intersect, this will be the <u>Township.</u> Now all you have to do is start with section #1 and count down to section 22. They will count like this. Start at #1 and count to the left to #6 section. Drop down and it will be #7. Count to the right six times and it will be #12. You continue doing this until you reach #22. Notice on the map the name <u>Pine.</u> This town will be somewhere in the mile section. Also notice after section #6 you'll see #1. This tells you this is another township. That's how easy it is to locate a ghost town in the county if you have the directions.

SAMPLE MAP

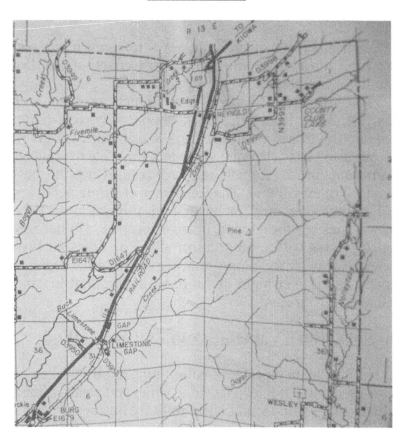

How to Clean Your Finds

I've heard a lot of different ways to clean items and I've tried most of them, but the most effective way I've found is a tumbler and electrolysis.

I use a tumbler I bought from "Finch products P.O. box 213, Birch Run, MI, 48415-Phone: (517) 624-9489. I've had the tumbler for ten years and it still runs great. Finch also has cleaning powder that cleans silver, aluminum, brass, copper and bronze and it's the best cleaner I've ever found. They also have cleaning pellets.

The blue ones are for silver and aluminum and the brown ones are for copper, brass or bronze. Do not mix copper, brass with aluminum or silver or they will turn brown. Clean silver alone and also aluminum alone. I usually ran it over night and it does an excellent job and will not pit your item.

Do Not Clean a Valuable Coin By This Method

Have it cleaned professional or none at all. A token or brass object will not lose its value when you clean it but a valuable coin will. Do not clean military buttons or it will lose its value.

Tip: don't clean nickels in brown pellets or it will turn brown and if you clean it in blue pellets it turns a dull aluminum color. Toss a few junk silver coins in with the nickels and use blue pellets and it will come out natural.

After cleaning and it's still not clean enough, I use a electrolysis cleaner. On iron I have used electrolysis cleaner, but it takes a long time but it will take the corrosion off. Through trial and error I have found a better way to clean iron. How about a sand blaster? Not the commercial kind but the kind you buy for your air compressor at home.

I once had an old iron bank that was covered with corrosion and rust. There was dull, faded white paint underneath the rust and I didn't want to take the paint off. I used 40 lb pressure and by using slow strokes ran it across the bank and checked it after each stroke. (Do not let the sand blaster stay stationery or it will pit it) If you take light strokes across it and check after each stroke, you can take the rust and corrosion off and leave the paint. Experiment with a corroded piece of iron before attempting this on the item you want to keep. Believe me it works, but experiment first.

Tumbler and Cleaning Pellets

Old Stage Route

How to Build a Simple Electrolysis Cleaner

Things needed:
  1- 12 volt power supply
  2- Set of red and black jumper leads
  3- Solder gun and solder

Go to radio shack or Wal-Mart and buy a 12 volt power supply the kind you use on a portable radio or CD player. (Do not use a car battery, it has too much current and will destroy your item) The 12 volt power supply you buy at Wal-Mart or radio supply has low current and will clean most items. Take a red clip lead and solder it to the positive lead of the power supply. Take a black clip lead and solder it to the negative lead of the power supply.

On the black lead, clip on another jumper lead that you will put in the water with the item you'll be cleaning. The clip in the water will eventually be eaten up and it's easier to replace the lead rather than solder another one on.

Enlisted Man's Button Cir: 1854 – 1902   Carved Lead Heart

How to Clean With Electrolysis Cleaner

Take a small plastic bowl such as a butter dish or whipped cream bowl and fill it almost full of warm or hot water. Take the red lead (Positive) and clip it onto a stainless steel spoon. Bend the spoon so it will fit on the edge of the plastic bowl with the spoon part in the water. Like this:

Keep the red lead (Positive) out of the water. (Do not let the spoon touch the black lead) clip the black lead (Negative) to the item you're cleaning and put it in the water. Drop a tablespoon of salt into the warm or hot water. Plug the power supply into the AC outlet. The item to be cleaned will start to bubble. If you have it backwards the spoon will bubble, simply reverse the red and black leads.

The water will begin to turn black or brown. This is the corrosion being released. Let it run for 45 minutes to an hour. (Warning: if you let it run for four or five hours or over night, it will eat the item up) Only run an hour at a time and check it. Take item out and brush with fine steel wool#00. This should take most if not all of the corrosion off.

If it's badly corroded repeat for another hour and check, but most of the items will clean in an hour. **Tip:** if you happen to clean an item and it's too clean and you want to darken it, here's how: Simply reverse the red and black leads, but watch it closely for it turns dark very quickly. Then lightly brush with steel wool and it will highlight the letters or figure. After cleaning rinse in clear water and dry.

Little Orphan Annie's Secret Society

<u>Step by Step Guide</u>

1- Name of Ghost Town you'd like to hunt.
2- Look in book: "Oklahoma Place Names" read brief history of town.
3- Look in: "Town and Place Locations" for exact directions to town.
4- Mark site on map along with other Ghost Town sites.
5- Go to location and see if you want to hunt it.
6- Go to nearest house and find landowner
7- Get permission
8- Hunt! Hunt! Hunt!

Otto Steinke * Good for 2 ½ Cents

Cleaned with Tumbler

After   Before

Cleaned with Electrolysis

Before   After

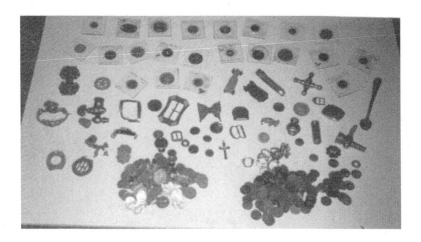

Misc. Items found

A few hunting buddies, Tinker Browning, Dan Pierce, Gordon Gibson, at Cabin Creek.

No, this is not the Boston Strangler-a buddy, Jim Kellogg

Mark Foreman with a nice Gotebo, Oklahoma token

Mark Foreman and I checking things out

"I know it's there somewhere! I'll find it!"

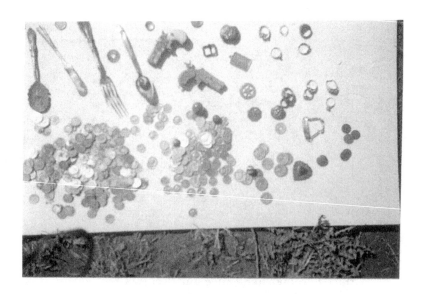

More items found in ghost towns

This is the old town site of Brinkman, Oklahoma (1910-1965)

The site of Tedda, Oklahoma (1904-1913) near the Canadian river.

"Sometimes you have to hunt where you can."

Hunting the ghost town site of Lockridge, Oklahoma (1903-1928)

See the glass? Good sign a dump is nearby

Unlisted Oklahoma Tokens

A.C. Aborn * Omega, OK. Ter.
50 Cents * Alum. * Value Unknown
25 Cents * Alum. * $435.00
5 Cents * Alum. * Value Unknown

This is A.C. Aborn's store in Omega, OK. Terr. (1893)

L. D. & J. C. Smith, Omega, Okla.

5 Cents * Alum. * Value Unknown

<u>Wadsworth Bros. * Omega, Oklahoma</u>

5 Cents * Alum * Value Unknown

<u>Smith Mercantile * Omega, Okla.</u>

5 Cents * Brass * Value Unknown

L.R. Anglin * Antlers, Okla.

50 cents * Alum. * Value unknown

W.K. Odhlrich * Hugo, Okla.

5 cents * Brass * Value unknown

<u>Ryan & Ryan * Billiard Parlor, Okemah, Okla.</u>

5 cents * Alum. * Value $200.00

<u>W. D. Hall * Brinkman, Oklahoma</u>

$1.00 * Brass * Value Unknown

Lockridge, Oklahoma (1903-1928)

On April 22, 1889, Ananias and Adeline Lenhart made the land run into central Oklahoma's unassigned lands and staked a homestead in Southwest Logan Country. The family lived in a dugout for six years while improving their claim. Ananias and his son "John Joseph" were instrumental in establishing the town of Lockridge. J. J. Lenhart ran a store from 1903-1928 at Lockridge. All that is left of this once thriving and prosperous town is a large plowed field.

J.J.Lenhart * Lockridge, Okla.
$1.00 * Alum. * Value $50.00
25 cents * Alum * Value $50.00
10 cents * Alum. * Value $40.00

W.E. Johnson * Lockridge, Okla.

50 Cents * Alum. * Value $50.00
25 Cents * Alum. * Value $50.00
10 Cents * Alum. * Value $35.00

Oklahoma & Indian Territory Tokens

Reed & Storm Gen. Merchants * Afton, Ind. Terr.

Bungalow Hotel & Bath House * Claremore, Okla.

J.V.C. Centralia, I.T. * Good for 5 cents

Oklahoma & Indian Territory Tokens

Renfro Drug Co. * Guthrie, O.T.

Walker & Livingston * Afton, I. T.

McAlester Coal Mining Co. * Buck Junction, I.T.

Watch Fobs

Army Items

SWASTIKA
COAL & COKE
"BEST FROM THE WEST"

SWASTIKA FUEL
COMPANY
RATON, NEW MEXICO

NEW MODERN DAIRY
GLOBE, ARIZONA

1 QUART
SPECIAL MILK

BRAHMA
BAR
WHEATLAND, WYO.

25¢
IN TRADE

Are you a Treasure Hunter?

A treasure hunter means different things to many people. Most people think of treasure hunters as someone who searches for treasure chests in the bottom of the ocean, Inca gold in the jungles of South America, or gold nuggets in the frozen land of Alaska. These are treasure hunters, but they are a minority. Most people search for treasure on the weekend because of job restrictions and time. We search for treasure a piece at a time. A coin here, a token there and sometimes we find a small cache. On any given weekend, you will see someone in a park, schoolyard or at an old abandoned lot enjoying this great hobby of metal detecting. However, if you also search for old furniture, books, toys, bottles, this is also treasure hunting.

I know I've been some kind of a treasure hunter all my life. Way back and I mean way back, when I was a lad of six, my brother, sister and I would go to the local dump. In those days, you could go to the dump and pick up anything there that you wanted. We were looking for toys, pop bottles and funny books. (That's what they use to call comic books) In the stores when they didn't sell the funny books, they would tear off the front covers and throw them away. I had one of the largest collections of funny books with no front cover and it was just as exciting to look at them whether it had a cover or not. In fact, even after fifty-five years I still have a few of them left. I don't know how I held on to them through all those years, but somehow I did.

We would also find many toys at the dump. It didn't matter that the Iron horse only had three legs or that the tricycle didn't have a front wheel. We were happy to find them. Although it was awful hard to ride a tricycle without a front wheel, somehow we did.

Our favorite toys were the ones we made ourselves. I used to take old Prince Albert tobacco cans, tear the lid off, and straddle it with my fingers. My fingers became a cowboy's legs and the can became my horse. I spent many hours and rode many miles in the backyard underneath the tall shade trees with one of these.

We would also take the largest tin cans we could find and run bailing wire though the top and stand on them. Holding tight on the wire so we wouldn't fall we would run races. There were many falls, but after a while we became quite proficient at this.

We also made our own rubber band guns. We'd cut a piece of wood into the shape of a pistol and wire a clothespin on the back. We didn't have rubber bands, so we cut car tubes into strips and stretched it as tight as we could. When you were shot it would leave a small red spot that would linger for days. They wouldn't call this fun now days, but back then it was a red badge of courage.

There was an old man named Buck who used to go to the dump every day. He drove an old beat up pickup and would search all day long looking for things to sale. We would always try to beat him to the dump for we were afraid he'd find out treasures. One day he found an old coin. He knew the local grocer was a coin collector, so he took it to him and he bought it for eighty dollars. Back then, eighty dollars was two months wages. Years Later, I found out it was a silver dollar, an 1804 silver dollar. One of these sold in 1989 for $220,000 dollars. That must have been one happy grocer when he acquired that coin. Back then the coin wasn't worth that much, but all in all that's not a bad return for an eighty dollar investment. Old Buck was a treasure hunter and in a roundabout way, so was the grocer. They both were searching for something and both made the find of a lifetime.

In our search for treasure one of our goals was to find five pop bottles each. The grocer would give us two cents for each bottle. This was a whopping ten cents. We would spend it on five-cent pop, two cents worth of tom's peanuts (from a machine) and three cents on penny candy. If this don't make you want to hunt treasure, I don't know what would. We would pour the peanuts in the pop and every time you took a drink you'd eat a peanut. We were happier then a dog with a bone.

My favorite pop was a brand called Virginia Dare. It was one of the first chocolate sodas. All of the chocolate would settle in the bottom of the bottle with a layer of clear unknown liquid on the top. You'd have to shake it up to mix the chocolate, but it was well worth it. We'd shake the devil out of it, giggling all the while. This was half the fun, shaking it up and it went down real smooth. I can still see all three of us, setting on the sidewalk on main street, laughing, and enjoying our goodies. It was a magical time.

As I grew in my teens, I developed new interest. I discovered girls, and I liked them. This was sort of a treasure hunt for you never know what you'd find. In the sixties, I discovered treasure hunting again when I saw a man in a park finding coins with this money finder and I have been hunting every since.

A friend of mine ran an ad in the paper to clean out garages, attics, and basements free for the things that were there. He would take the items to the flea market, sell them and did quite well. Later, he moved out of town and I decided to try this unique form of treasure hunting. I ran an ad in the paper and I never hauled so much free trash in my life. I found out real quick, this was not my kind of treasure hunting although it paid off for him. All I got out of it was a lot of dump fees and a sore back.

Everybody can't ride the same horse and sometimes you have to step back and punt, which I did.

The greatest treasure I found was in 1959, when I found my dear wife Elsie. We've been married for 49 years and two of them were happy. (Just kidding honey) Are you a treasure hunter? If you're looking for money, happiness, love, security, then you're searching for something and if you're searching for something then you're a treasure hunter whether you know it or not. Welcome to my world, the world of treasure hunting.

Roy Rogers Belt Bucket

GOOD FOR
ONE CAKE
PALMOLIVE
SOAP FREE
WHEN YOU BUY
ONE CAKE

FREE
10 CENT CAKE
JAP ROSE
WHEN   TWO
YOU BUY   CAKES
KIRK'S FLAKE
SOAP
WITH THIS
CHECK

TO DEALERS
THIS CHECK WILL BE
REDEEMED AT YOUR
RETAIL PRICE AND ONLY
WHEN CONDITIONS ON
THE REVERSE SIDE HAVE
BEEN COMPLIED WITH
THE PALMOLIVE-PEET CO
CHICAGO
P-1009

DEALERS:
WE WILL REDEEM
THIS CHECK AT YOUR
RETAIL PRICE WHEN YOU HAVE
COMPLIED   WITH
CONDITIONS   STATED
ON REVERSE SIDE
JAMES S. KIRK & CO.
CHICAGO,
ILL.

Frank Hayslip

Frank has hunted ghost towns for over twenty years and has been a member of the Twin Territories Treasure Hunters Club since 1996. He has served as vice-president and board member and has written several articles for Lost Treasure and Western and Eastern Treasure magazines. When asked once to summarize his life he said, "When I was fifteen, I rode a freight train to California, hitched-hiked back. Joined the Marine Corp to see the world and spent four years in the Mojave Desert. Been shot at and missed, got married, ran a bar, played in a band, wrote songs, cut a record, have three wonderful children and have been married to the same woman for over forty-nine years. Through thick and thin, knock down and drag out, I kept her and I'm glad I did. Who else would wash my clothes, fix me something to eat and tell me how pretty I am."

160 pages * $19.95

For twenty-nine years the author has searched for lost treasure with a metal detector. His search has led him from the panhandle of Oklahoma to the Wichita Mountains in Southwestern Oklahoma hunting abandon homesteads, ghost towns, army camps, cache hunting, and Spanish Treasures. His stories are told in this book along with true stories of other treasure hunters, many tips, where to look, and lots of photos of his finds. Also in this book is a collection of his stories first published in *Lost Treasure & Western & Eastern Treasure Magazine* of his adventures while metal detecting. If you're interested in all types of treasure hunting then this book is for you.

Made in the USA
Middletown, DE
07 June 2022

66825558R00040